The Patient Body

The Patient Body

A PERSONAL NARRATIVE

in pieces

SEBASTIAN MATTHEWS

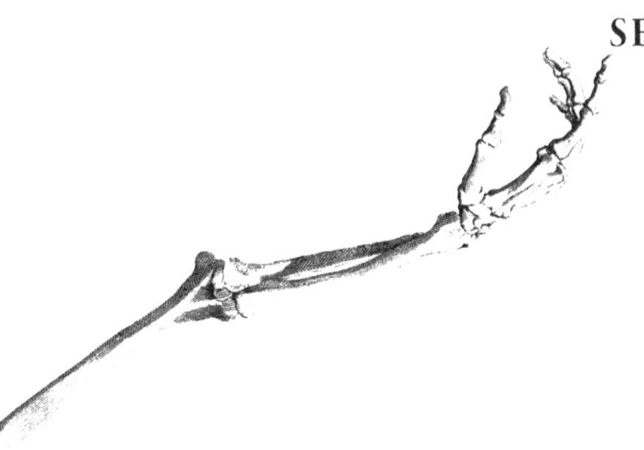

Red Hen Press | *Pasadena, CA*

The Patient Body

Book design by Mark E. Cull.

Library of Congress Cataloging-in-Publication Data

Names: Matthews, Sebastian, 1965– author.
Title: The patient body: a personal narrative in pieces/ Sebastian Matthews.
Description: First edition. | Pasadena: Red Hen Press, 2025.
Identifiers: LCCN 2024019879 (print) | LCCN 2024019880 (ebook) | ISBN 9781636282442 (trade paperback) | ISBN 9781636282466 (hardcover) | ISBN 9781636282459 (ebook)
Subjects: LCSH: Matthews, Sebastian, 1965– | Authors, American—21st century—Biography. | Traffic accident victims—United States—Biography. | Essays. | LCGFT: Essays. | Autobiographies.
Classification: LCC PS3613.A853 A6 2025 (print) | LCC PS3613.A853 (ebook) | DDC 811/.6 [B]—dc23/eng/20240722
LC record available at https://lccn.loc.gov/2024019879
LC ebook record available at https://lccn.loc.gov/2024019880

The National Endowment for the Arts, the Los Angeles County Arts Commission, the Ahmanson Foundation, the Dwight Stuart Youth Fund, the Max Factor Family Foundation, the Pasadena Tournament of Roses Foundation, the Pasadena Arts & Culture Commission and the City of Pasadena Cultural Affairs Division, the City of Los Angeles Department of Cultural Affairs, the Audrey & Sydney Irmas Charitable Foundation, the Meta & George Rosenberg Foundation, the Albert and Elaine Borchard Foundation, the Adams Family Foundation, Amazon Literary Partnership, the Sam Francis Foundation, and the Mara W. Breech Foundation partially support Red Hen Press.

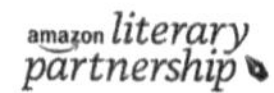

First Edition
Published by Red Hen Press
www.redhen.org

Acknowledgments

The below prose pieces appeared, often under different titles, in the following publications:

Journals
Asheville Poetry Review: "Imminence"; *Cortland Review*: "The Patient Body Disguised as a Church Fire"; *Ecotone*: "End of Summer"; *Hole in the Head Review*: "The Patient Body Looks at Itself in a Funhouse Mirror," "The Patient Body Wanders into Applebee's"; *Literary Matters*: "At the Frida Kahlo Museo," "Microfiche," "VW Litany"; *Orion*: "Walking Walden Pond, Its Paths Now Fenced In By Wire"; *Provincetown Arts Magazine*: "Kamasi Washington at the Orange Peel"; *Symposeum*: "The Patient Body Gets an MRI."

Anthologies
Crossing the Rift—North Carolina Poets on 9-11 & Its Aftermath: "The Patient Body on the Day Everything Changed"; *I Wanna Be Loved by You—Poems on Marilyn Monroe*: "The Night Ella Escorted Marilyn through the Front Door of the Mocambo"; *Token Entry—New York Subway Poems*: "Broadway."

Pamphlet Series
Longhouse Publishing: "Battenkill," "Best of the Classic Years," "Microfiche," "News."

Thanks go to:
Bob Arnold, Mildred Barya, Joseph Bathanti, Curtis Bauer, Tina Cane, Susanne H. Case, Gary Clark, Camille Dungy, Melissa Febos, Keith Flynn, Vievee Francis, Glenn Freeman, Landon Godfrey, Christine Hale, Luke Hankins, Marie Harris, Gary Hawkins, Michael Hettich, Major Jackson, Richard Jackson, Aviya Kushner, Gerry LaFemina, Dana Levin, Andrew Najberg, James Navé, Gregory Pardlo, Jason Schneiderman, Bill Shulz, Margo Taft Stever, Brit Washburn, Ryan Walsh, Ryan Wilson, & the late great Kevin McIlvoy.

And even more thanks to:
All the good folks at the Vermont Studio Center; *Callaloo*; Erin Hallagan Clare at Story Parlor; Rachel Hanson and the crew at Punch Bucket Lit; Lily Danzis and Jennifer McGaha at the Great Smokies Writing Program at UNC-Asheville; Heather Newton and Maggie Marshall at Flatiron Writers Room; Davyne Dial at WPVM; and Gary Lilley, Eric Greenwell, Marie George & the crew at the Port Townsend Writers Conference.

Big tip of the hat to all of my students at Great Smokies and my one-on-one clients.

Big bow of appreciation to Tobi Harper, Monica Fernandez, Shelby Wallace, Rebeccah Sanhueza, Kate Gale, Mark E. Cull, and the entire Red Hen crew.

Much love and gratitude to Ali, my partner in life, to whom I owe so much.

for Avery

Contents

Friend

The Patient Body

Neighbor

Citizen

Traveler

Artist

The Patient Body

Preface

It seems now as if the accident occurred a lifetime ago, made to seem even longer by the anesthetizing span of the pandemic. In fact, it is coming on fourteen years since my family was nearly killed in that head-on collision. I am about to turn 60, Ali is 55, and our son is in his early 20s. That newly middle-aged man I was back in 2011 seems a whole other person, almost a stranger. Still, there are days the accident feels like it just happened. I can still feel it in my bones.

In *Beginner's Guide to a Head-On Collision*, my attention was focused on both the event itself and its aftermath. In *Beyond Repair: Living in a Fractured State*, I turned away from my own personal trauma and moved out into the world only to find my inner life mirrored by society's own brand of post-traumatic stress. And now, in this third book in what has become a kind of trilogy, *The Patient Body: A Personal Narrative in Pieces*, the subject has become, simply put, the body. The body, and what it means to be alive in the present while remembering the past and looking to the future. The *healing* body, and what it means to be a survivor of a devasting crash—as husband, father, friend, neighbor, citizen, etc. What it means to live an *embodied* life. And then: what—and who—one encounters when one moves out into the world. The encounter, an essential part of daily life; one of the patient body's best and oldest teachers.

A friend once wrote that an auto accident "cleaves a life," moving it "into *before* and *after*." I'd add that it breaks a life into pieces. To get back into your life—to get your body back—you have to work hard to pick up those pieces and work harder still to fashion a new way of being. *One can return*, a line in a song goes, and I am paraphrasing, *just not all the way*. Why do I find that truth so soothing? Maybe because there's no such thing as returning all the way, but only the best we can muster, in and among our family and friends, in these difficult times.

—Asheville, NC
Spring, 2025

. . . Something like
the body of the poet's work, with its
pale shadows, begins to pare and replace
the poet's body, and isn't it time?

—"On a Diet," William Matthews

Young Man

Emilio's

I remember slipping down the steep stairs with money in hand to order an Italian sub. I was there in part to watch Emilio slice the meat—first the salami, then the ham. He'd be chatting the whole time, looking over his shoulder as he passed the blade across the slab of meat, one hand cupped under the blade to catch the thin pieces as they dropped. It seemed like a magic trick that he didn't slice his fingers off. I am thinking about all this now because I just ordered an Italian sub from a local sub shop, and the oil and vinegar they use (with added spices and parmesan cheese) sends me back there on an olfactory magic carpet ride. Not so much a granted wish as a surprising gift. Brother Willy, he was Willy then, had the bottom bunk. I slept up top. On Saturday mornings I could peer down on Daniel Street and monitor the foot traffic. Emilio standing out on the stoop, still wearing his dirtied apron. People stopping to chat; the little bell ringing when they stepped inside. Sound of door knocking back into place. Cigarette smoke slipping into the window like a cartoon snake. I am right back there: the tangy smell of orange soda, the scratchy pop tunes emanating from the portable radio behind the counter. Emilio's handsome, mustachioed face floating in the mirror.

—Portsmouth, New Hampshire, 1973

End of Summer

All Alan wanted to do that last summer was go over to John's and smoke cigarettes with his friends. We'd wait until John's mom backed her car out of the drive—she had the late shift at the county hospital—then start rustling around in the pantry. If we got lucky, there would be a few cans of warm beer or some cooking sherry, and we'd kill the rest of the night up in his drafty barn loft out behind their ramshackle house, shooting the shit and listening to Zeppelin and Hendrix. The whole summer seemed to go that way. In a few days we'd all be starting high school—Alan a Catholic school over in Concord, John the local public school, me all the way across the country in Seattle. I couldn't have articulated the feeling then, but I remember the whole summer having this sense that something big needed to happen—that Alan and I had to make it happen—before it was too late. Before *what* was too late? I wasn't sure. Before the summer ended maybe, and with it my childhood. As if a screen door might somehow slam shut in the wind and mysteriously latch.

—Barnstead, New Hampshire, 1978

Volunteer Park

Though I've seen the men standing inside the grove of trees before—a dozen or more, each leaning against his own tree—it takes me a while to figure what's going on. I walk past them after a game of tennis or on my way out for a reservoir run. A few nods, but mostly they look away. One man comes out of the low cement building and slips off into the shadows; on cue, another leaves his tree and slips inside. Sometimes two men go into the public bathroom together. Sometimes the man who walks in isn't the man who walks out. Every few minutes, another man in, another man out. Is it the same men again and again, or do they take new partners each time? Is it just blow jobs and hand jobs or straight up fucking? In the stalls? Against the sink and mirrors? Do they wear condoms? Is money exchanged? Once a cop car pulls up and everyone silently disperses. When a man approaches, I sputter something and run off. All summer I keep returning, hovering around the edges of this half circle of silent men, eventually turning away and leaving, unwilling or unable to join them.

—Seattle, Washington, 1982

Broadway

In the city to visit the old man. Slouching through Penn Station, pack heavy on slender back, sweat streaming down my shirt into a ratty pair of cargo pants. It's late, the station simmers its subterranean stew. I'm struggling to keep pace with the frenetic crowd, don't want to gawk like a tourist tripping between signs—swerving from red circle to red circle, sneaking jaw drops at all the ridiculously stylish people floating by. There's graffiti everywhere, marking every surface. A downtown 1 train drawing its brakes is blanketed in a scrawl of tags, smothered in a rainbow of bravado. Some glorious soul in a Bernard King jersey plays the cello in a corner as a pair of young men drum madly on overturned buckets, seeing who will expire first—the echoes bouncing inside converging bodies. The smell of piss and sweat mix with low-tar cigarettes and wafts of perfume; then a pounding cascade of steps down to the platform. Here, too, bodies are jammed together, which means an advanced scout of squeaks and flashes will soon whip around the curve in an arc of headlight (illuminating the night's latest spray paint smears). But for now everyone's just occupying space, insolent in that elusive way of New Yorkers, as if each moment is a blind audition for the star part. A little sorrow inside the gusto, a tiny leak in the back tire as the group of friends sets out on a summer jaunt out to the beaches . . . The *hiss* of doors opening. Squeezing into an open seat between old Walker Evans women who smell of gin and stale crackers. The car rocking us to the edge of sleep . . . *103rd . . . 110th . . . 116th . . . Next stop 125th & Broadway . . .*

—Manhattan, 1985

Microfiche

Junior year of college I moved out of the dorms, answering an ad for a small two-bedroom pad a few blocks from town. My roommate a grad student and a bit of a hermit. It took a month for him to tell me his dissertation was on the Dead Sea Scrolls. A living room cabinet full of microfiche slides in stacks. He talked about them for hours. That was the closest we got. He moved out by semester's end. A girlfriend moved in, then my brother, back from Santa Fe, and the place became a salon of sorts, parties cropping up every weekend. A honkytonk quartet lived behind us. The lead singer, gorgeous and kind, would come over after fights with her old man. We'd get her stoned. She'd sing the opening chorus from that big Peggy Lee hit and eat our spaghetti. My brother moved out and soon I did too. But what a wild place, never more so, I see now, than when the slides were lined up on the floor, fragment by ancient fragment, and a shy scholar tried to give a young poet a glimpse into that incendiary world of ghosts. Breathing each letter to life, picking up then setting down the flimsy microfiche slides. I am surprised the whole place didn't burn down.

—Claremont, California, 1987

Battenkill

The trees shrug off their robes in little waves of wind, leaves dropping in the current. The river awash in cockeyed light. I take off shoes and socks and stack river rocks into wobbly towers. Two shadowy trout slip around my ankles then disappear. There's a book open on a boulder, pen and paper. Time a bowl of light.

—Ripton, Vermont, 1991

Nights Around the Welcome Table

When I started graduate school in Ann Arbor, the novelist Nicholas Delbanco was the University of Michigan's MFA program director. I had known him since I was a teen, having met him and his family up at the Bread Loaf Writers Conference a decade before. He was the main reason I chose UM. Near the start of my second year, he invited me and Ali—newly together, soon to be engaged—to what he called his *welcome table*, quoting James Baldwin, who had been friendly to him when he was just starting out as a young novelist. "We talked as most writers do," Delbanco told me. "In a kind of shorthand and sign language." That first dinner, we were made to feel that we'd be the sole guests for a special meal. Arriving appropriately dressed, excited, a bottle of wine as thank you gift, we were surprised to find a sitting room full of guests, wine glasses in hand, and a large table decked out for the fabulous meal to come. We were fooled a second time by Nick and Elena's seemingly personal invite, more than a little late in realizing that for Nick, as for Baldwin, a table wasn't truly welcome until brimming with a "full retinue of intimates." To be invited at all was to be taken seriously, and to be included in the grand master's party was to be accepted into that age-old bohemian club of writers and artists, and to belong.

—Ann Arbor, Michigan, 1994

Husband

Hallelujah

We drove into the snowstorm as if entering an alternate reality—a cinematic wipe shuttling us into a silver landscape of snow and ice. That "Hallelujah" came on a few beats after—Jeff Buckley's opening breath a puff of fog on the windshield—only added to the surprise. Whatever we were before, we were wide awake now. We shared a glance, not wanting to jinx it. I placed my hands firm but light on the wheel, worried that this was all too good, that too much joy too all of a sudden might just upend our lives and spill them down the mountainside. We were on the Blue Ridge Parkway, up on that snaking track winding slowly to the top of Mt. Mitchell. There'd been not a whiff of snow back in town. We had fallen silent a few switchbacks back. In Buckley's cover, there are quite a few drifting, near silences, lightly strummed chords hanging in the air, drawn-out syllables in choir boy falsetto morphing into tormented wails. I'd cracked the window. Ali's eyes were closed. She was taking it in through her pores. This was less than a year before our son entered our lives. We were young, still in love with our love. And it was before television and movies had laid Cohen's eerily lovely song all over their climactic scenes like syrup, ruining it for anything else but hyperbole. I can remember the blue-black slick of road leading us through the snow-covered trees, shrunken and hunched by years of wind, and the sound of the tires on wet asphalt. How Ali opened her eyes and stared down the valley on our left, her hand warm on my forearm. And how, when we dropped low enough in altitude, the winter snow, as quickly as it had appeared, vanished.

Together

Avery has just turned one. And though my father has been dead now for seven years, there are times late at night, alone in my study, when I pick up the phone and start dialing, hoping to share the latest news. It takes a moment to realize he is no longer on the other end of the late-night line. Hard to comprehend that, though I am still his son, he is not around to be my father. In moments like this I understand just how important it is to be there for Avery—as long as we can and in every way possible. In the last years before my father died, our relationship as father and son transformed dramatically. We'd both found partners with whom we hoped to settle. Each planned to stay in one place for more than a few years. But somehow the roles had reversed. All of a sudden, my father was looking to me—to my marriage with Ali in particular—and seeing the apparent stability I'd found with her as something to strive for. I mean really hope for. That maybe I had become, in some small way, his role model for a new way of life. Though I'm unsure he was really going to make it that way. (How could he have? It had never worked before. And rarely, barely, for me.) At the funeral, one of his best friends told me that my father already had one foot out the door. *He kept making promises he couldn't keep.* I don't know. All I know is how happy his grandson would have made my father. How content I'd have been watching them shoot hoops together.

Snow Day

Picture the scene. Snow falling softly, no wind, not too cold. Picture the sky a cool curtain of gray. Car in the driveway dusted with a layer of wet snow. Now a winter-jacketed man comes out and begins changing the car's tire. A dog, let out to romp in the snow, runs off to relieve herself under a tree. A house guest comes out, hat on his head, here to help change the tire. Inside, a mother dresses her boy who has been at the window, mouth to cold glass, watching the men. The boy joins the scene, wandering around the yard happily, tasting snow off the tip of his gloves. The father struggles to jack up the car, two tires in a pile. A neighbor's daughter appears, decked out in snow pants and bright red gloves. The dog runs in mad circles, kicking up snow. The mother stays inside and makes herself a cup of coffee. Outside, the snow has turned to sleet-snow. When the dog grabs one of the girl's gloves and tears around the yard, the man follows behind, mock growling. The boy climbs along the fence imagining a great fall below, arms out like a high-wire walker. The second tire on. The snow starts to stick again. Eventually hands get cold, and everyone heads inside. The mother puts in a video for the kids. Sections of the Sunday paper grabbed up. The dog clumping down by the fire. Logs collapsing in on themselves.

First Day of School

Avery stands at the opening of our dead-end street in the still dark morning, his new school shoes flashing orange as we kick the soccer ball back and forth. The first day of kindergarten. Picture Day. He insists you dress him in his new collared shirt for the occasion. He wants to send cards to Nana and Papa, Mimi and Charter, his cousin Kira. He's written them each a little note, has spelled out the words all by himself. And in each he wants to include one of his watercolor drawings. And, and, and . . . And the bus is coming down the hill, brights on, brakes hissing. And when you run your hand through Avery's hair, he knocks it away. *Mom!* He climbs up the vibrating steps without using the rail for balance. His driver, Miss Rita, watches attentively, waving to us before letting the door close. As the big yellow bus pulls off, we wave at the blank windows, catching only a glimpse of our son framed in the glass. He's waving back, but we can't tell if he's smiling or frowning. And then he's gone.

A Lifetime, in Three Acts

1.

Floating in clouds of anesthesia and painkillers in hospital rooms two hours apart. You were driven up the mountain back to Asheville; I, still stuck in the car, finally got helicoptered out just before the storm hit. Both of us relieved to be alive, too tired to say much more than *Love you.* When Avery was brought to visit, he seemed surprised to see me sitting up in bed, made nervous by all the nurses and wires and by the large circles under my eyes. He laughed easily at my lame jokes and wanted to see my stitches. Only eight years old, Avery walked out of the car unharmed except for one stark seatbelt bruise etched across his chest.

2.

After two relentless weeks, two surgeries, they strapped me in the back of a van and carted me up the mountain to a rehab center near our house. The whole ride I was jostled and bumped in my seat, though the driver couldn't (or wouldn't) hear my fearful complaints. They placed me in a room with two beds. Within a few days, you joined me. We dubbed the room "the honeymoon suite." Beds pushed close. Avery spent afternoons with us. He piled into bed with us to watch some movie. It didn't matter which. Friends and neighbors floated in to see our faces and left vases of overly aromatic flowers.

3.

Discharge day. A long wooden ramp led up to our front door where steps used to be. Our dog's tail thumped the ground. Neighbors had stocked the fridge with food. The bed moved down to the living room. Avery showed us around the new digs, beaming. It was all too much. When everyone left, we extracted ourselves from our wheelchairs and laid down on our bed, overcome with emotion. Avery dragged his bed down and placed it at the foot of ours. The dog stayed close to our sides. The walls were covered in get-well cards. A lifetime since we'd all been together, since last sleeping in our own bed.

Forgiveness

In the dream you approach nervously, your face a blend of anticipation and grief. *There you are!* I can see everything in your eyes I have put you through. *Yes, here I am.* But where? I sit at a corner table whiting-out a letter I don't remember writing. You take hold of my hands. I say, *I'm sorry to have been gone so long.* I can see it is okay, that it's not okay and never will be. *Come back,* you say, *just for a little while.* It would be good. *It would.* When I stand up, I am naked, body as worn as a dollar. When I stand up, my entire life spills onto the ground. You say, *Come with me.*

Seesaw

Do you remember the night Avery brought out the folding table onto the porch for a night of card games with his buds? Was he fourteen? Fifteen? That old cliché about time passing in a blink. How he got dressed up, laid out a full board of snacks, pulled out special drinking glasses (not *those* glasses) then waited for his friends to show. How it broke our hearts a little and filled us with joy to see him host his friends in this manner. There was so much love there, but also a kind of acting out of how the future might look, how he wanted it to look. Sitting in the living room, listening to the happy rumblings outside, we couldn't help but feel a sharp sense of time teetering on a pivot, a tidal pulse flowing back and forth—one seesaw end dipping down into the past, the other rising up into the future.

Father

Convergence

Two bedraggled men camped out under a tree; a grocery cart parked behind them brimming with garbage bags stuffed with clothing. One snorted his disdain then got up and hobbled off to our left as we set our towels down atop a mossy rock. It was early. The place would be packed soon enough. An entertaining, always slightly chaotic weekend scene: whole families out with their dogs, groups of young shirtless men nursing coolers of beer and napping in the bushes. A man-made sluice had been built into the riverbank, huge stone slabs arranged on both sides. Young kids liked to wedge their bodies up into the tiny waterfall, letting the current pulse over them before letting go and being carried downstream. But that morning, water high from recent rainfall, the place was nearly empty. Avery and Phoenix took turns jumping off the rope swing, waiting until the top of the arc to let go (so as not to land on the two boulders visible in the water below). They dove for stray golf balls from the driving range upriver. One of the homeless men slipped off into the bushes. The other jumped into the muddy water, floating like a big white bear. "It's a bit nippy," he intoned happily. Friends of ours don't like coming to this spot. *It's not that I am racist but . . .* Me, I liked the funkiness of such intersection, the convergence of cultures and subcultures. Families started to arrive, climbing out of cars on the edge of the field, lugging plastic rings and towels and transistor radios, speaking to one another softly in Spanish. They'd stay until sundown.

At the Waffle House

Three line cooks. Three waitresses. Two managers—man facing customers, woman calling out orders, *smothered, covered, over easy, steak & eggs*. The left-side cook sets up plates, kept waffles coming. Right-side cook grills the meat, replaces the egg basket over the center cook's head as he turns out omelets, hash browns, eggs. The waitresses floats back and forth, setting down full plates, picking up empties, refilling coffees, bringing more toast for the previous night's prom goers (some still in their gowns and tuxes), for Avery's soccer team in their dirty uniforms slumped next to their rumpled dads, and for all the extra personnel in town for Military Week, line out the door. All I can think, as the manager listens to a waitress complain about some wrong and answers, "Communication is key"—meaning *I hear ya* and *I got your back*, but *now's not the time for any more of that,* and the waitress walks off, still fuming but nodding her head—is that we need more of this, whatever this is I am witnessing here in Greenville, North Carolina, nine thirty in the morning, the rain outside already beginning to sizzle a little on asphalt and all the lights turning green.

Beautiful Bonehead

A rallying cry uttered mutely in your body. Savage grace lacing itself up and releasing, lacing up and releasing. Skateboard kicked up (tunes thumping on speaker) and flipped, kicked up and flipped. Ball punted for ball-mad dog, for ball-mad dog. Warmed up bowl of last night's dinner, glass of milk, then back to your room. Pile of wet towels dropped in the hall. Standing at the top of the stairs, shower-wet, junk in hand, calling for a clean towel. Facetime, FIFA, Black Ops, Snapchat. Barefoot on the driveway waiting for your hookup to bring the pack. Six teenage boys at the kitchen table ravenous over pancakes. You text me to come up and wake you if you start pushing it. Beautiful bonehead, how can I protect you when I am camped in the far corner? What can I do but offer you a fist bump and say, *Love you, man.*

VW Bug Litany

> And what a shame they don't make *Los Suicidas* mescal anymore, what a shame that time passes, don't you think? What a shame that we die, and get old, and everything goes galloping away from us.
>
> —Roberto Bolaño, *The Savage Detectives*

The first parked along the dusty road just outside Akumal Bay's little downtown zocalo, dark green, tattooed with stickers, rusted chassis, the perfect beach town relic circa 1972 or '73, down from Mexico City or Merida, or as far away as San Diego or maybe even Austin, TX. The second driving the other way on the main thoroughfare (two lanes on either side, periodic *returnos* slotted in between the long string of resorts, each with its own Vegas-esque grand entry). This one as white as cream, near mint condition, gleaming tires, a flag of a car waving in the heat; the next a brilliant bright blue, like a strip of ocean at Playa del Carmen; then another—this one *in* Playa del Carmen—lime green, nearly neon, parked between a line of ratty scooters and a tourist van bound for the Coba ruins. It's covered in dirt, like a hologram from some other time, or a memory hallucinated by the old man crossing the street in a mariachi band costume, guitar almost dragging behind him he's so tired. There are enough of them that I keep a lookout—down back alleys and side streets, along the coastal highway we keep entering and exiting—just slightly obsessed with the idea of spotting another, and another—anywhere, everywhere—all in various states of disrepair, each its own homage to an earlier time less subsumed by consumerism, a *sui generous* emblem for a band of ghosts long since dispersed, bound for Chile or Ecuador. They remind me of the one sad Beetle left to rot in the middle of an old tennis court tucked into a nook somewhere in my grandparent's wealthy neighborhood (Rye, NY, circa 1972 or '73), itself gone to seed, the way things sometimes are: abandoned, the fence falling into itself in unobserved slow motion (glacial increments then, one day, a final sag to the ground); in the corner a tree growing up through the concrete, scrub oak or beech, I can't remember. Though I can see vividly the cousins swarming the court, lost in a wild 4-on-4 or 5-on-5 tennis scrum while I climb into the body of the abandoned VW, pretending to drive it on out of there, or maybe trying to referee the match swirling around me from inside its stripped carcass shell. The front seat a dangerous nest of wire and metal rods, the windows long since knocked out. A hole where the lighter used to be. Maybe, I can't entirely recall, one of the doors, freed from its hinges, is caught in the remnant of net laying like a snake across the cracked cement in amongst leaves, vines, empty cigarette packs and Narragansett beer cans, rusted like tiny cars without their wheels; nothing at all like the basketball court here at the center of town, Akumal Bay, with its cement supports and brightly colored geometries, peopled this lovely evening with a family of little kids, an old ball, and a dad trying to teach the eldest daughter how to dribble and shoot. One of the younger boys rides his scooter in rough circles as the last light drops behind the palms, now, the afternoon rain having brought down the heat a few notches, and the breeze off the ocean a caress on our necks and forearms—our little family, heading back from a dinner on the beach, heading for our rental, also a VW, but not at all like these old Volkswagens we keep stumbling upon. It's what we have for this little vacation we're on, this sweet little trip we have enjoyed so much, down here on the Mayan Riviera, despite having almost no Spanish, Avery restless, ready to hop into one and—windows open to the night wind, someone passing a joint back—catch a ride as far as it will take him, far away from us.

Shit Job

Six in the morning. I'm up, you aren't. Why is it that I feel the need to get you up when we both know you should be able to accomplish this simple task yourself? Learn to keep a job, to live your life on your own terms, even if wobbly with sleep-deprivation. Why am I up, tugging at your feet to make sure you're not going to fall back asleep as soon as I leave the room? I should just let you miss the shift—the manager already let me know in no uncertain terms I wasn't to call on your behalf or make excuses—and so lose the shit job you complain about for paying you so little. You need to feel that brand of pain in the ass radiating up your body like a sciatic nerve on fire. But I don't. And here I am, at 6:27 a.m., handing you a muffin with peanut butter. You stuff it in your mouth and mumble, *Let's go.* The dog shadows you, ready to climb in the backseat for the three-minute drive. You steal a hit off the vape device you know I hate, despite every warning and threat, and climb out of the car with a quiet *Thanks.* Then the brief drive home, climbing back in bed and, after burning through a set of well-worn worry tapes, eventually falling into a thin, fitful sleep.

Rising to the Bait

The lane is morphing into right-turn only. The truck behind doesn't see or pay attention to my blinker; just enough time and space to slip in without making the guy hit his breaks, but tight. I sit at the red light, the truck right up to the bumper. It sits too high to see the driver. I think: *Yeah, yeah, I should have waited for you to pass. But you should have let me in.* The light turns green and, when I go through the intersection, the truck follows, staying a little too close behind. I turn right, and the truck turns too. I'm heading to the sporting goods shop to get Avery something for his eighteenth birthday. Maybe I should have turned left at the stop sign and made my way to the correct lane and turned in there, but I am sick of having the truck on my tail so cut across the empty lot. I pull into the empty space next to Avery's car. He's been waiting for me. The truck speeds up just as I open the door, no more than a foot away. This angry white guy stares at me through the window. I raise my hands, palms up. *What the fuck?* By the time I've climbed out of the car, he's heading my way, now up in my face. He's a big white dude. I can see Avery looking over, curious what's going on. "Why did you do that?" "Do what?" "Open your door like that." "I didn't know you were pulling into the spot." "Yes, you did." I'm not backing down but not escalating either. My son's now walked into the picture, showing the guy there's two of us to contend with. I say, pointing at the storefront: "We're just trying to shop." "So am I," the guy says. I want to call bullshit—he isn't here to shop—but hold my tongue. Avery nods his head toward the store. *Come on, Dad*. After two long beats, the guy turns back to the truck. He snarls over his shoulder, "Next time I'll take off your fucking car door." When we get inside, I hover near the sliding doors until I see the truck drive off. "What was *that* about?" Avery asks. I shrug, at a loss for words.

Marking

There's a small one on your ankle you warned we might not like—a gun with a heart shooting from its muzzle. There's another, hidden away, your friend scratched into your skin drunk. On the inside of your forearm two tats in magnetic charge: full-color globe hovering over a wedge of triangular earth—or maybe it's a mountain—floating in space like an asteroid. Do they represent the way you see yourself? A testament to who you were then? The dog bite scar is its own form of tattoo, a mark you didn't choose but brands you nonetheless—a long purple line running across your arm, nearly piercing the globe. The charging Great Dane went for your neck; if it wasn't for your brute strength and quick wittedness, it might have finished the job. And what about the invisible scar the bad acid trip seared across your cerebellum? That night you came to us with empty eyes; we were robots, space aliens had stolen our souls. You weren't sure you could go on living. What else? There's the small Jewish star on your left hand middle finger in honor of your fallen hip-hop idol and the faith you were raised in. A fuck-you flag to wag at the world? And the one on the inside of your right forearm of a cartoon kid, squat and thick-lined, thumb up in an all's-well salute. A reminder that things will work out—despite it all, through it all, scars and all. That there might be a tomorrow.

Friend

Life Ball

I'm on a birding expedition with my buddy Jay. He's a serious birder; I am most definitely not. I start snapping shots of random things—park sculpture, a graffiti-covered road sign. When I spy an old tennis ball wedged deep into the bog marsh, I take a picture of it too. "Look, Jay," I say, handing over my camera phone. "It's a life ball!" Jay chuckles, handing it me back to me. He knows I am a smartass. My mother, an ardent birder, turned me onto the phrase "life bird" years back. It always seemed a little strange to me, a tad morbid. Still, I follow Jay, zooming in on the shot with that particular two-finger spread. "A Wilson 7. That's rare." Jay ignores me, his binoculars up to his eyes. He is staring instead at a tree across the lake, trying to match the call he heard to a particular branch. "Another Carolina Wren," he confirms, adjusting the binoculars' focus. I can't let it go. "They stopped using that shade of yellow after the 7, you know." And I keep up the less and less amusing banter all the way around the south end of the lake. We return to the car. Jay is busy arranging his gear in the back. "Nothing new," he says to himself. I whisper, "It's the Penn 3 I'm really after."

Sesame Seed Bagel

Three friends in town early morning. In a few hours two of us are heading home, flying off in separate directions, while the other drives country roads back to work. Ryan has brought us to this Montreal-rooted bagel joint tucked away in a warehouse district. The tiny space consists of a long counter, a couple of booths, a picnic table. Big ovens line the back wall. After ordering bagels with smear, we sit at a table, talk of the last few shared days—of all the projects picked up, discussed, brought forward in small steps. Curtis looks at his watch. Almost time to go. All of a sudden, a lofted bagel appears—its unexpected arrival signaled by a doughy waft—on the end of a ridiculously long wooden paddle. It floats there a moment then, with a flick of the baker's wrist, slides off into the basket. "Try this," the baker barks across the counter, smiling broadly. I tear the bagel into thirds and pass around the steaming bread. Dark seeds fall to the table.

—Burlington, VT

Specific

Down for breakfast in the hotel, early, I pull a menu from the basket. The hostess says, "Party of one?" I look around for my friends. "No, a group of us." She smiles: "You're the first. Right this way." She gestures toward an empty dining room. "I guess I'll come back." I head for the lobby to text my friends. After ten minutes, still no answer, hungry, I decide to grab a seat. They'll find me. This time the hostess leads me into the bar area. I spot my friends at a corner table, nearly done with their breakfast. I turn, pointing, throwing the hostess an incredulous look. "Those are my friends!" She seems surprised. "I didn't know you were together." I leave her standing there and walk over to the table in a huff. When I tell my friends what happened, they smile sadly, shaking their heads. This is not uncommon. I am white. My friends are Black. "Maybe," Greg says, hand on my arm, "you needed to specify."

—Providence, RI

Dear Friend,

I wish things had gone differently. That your question didn't feel like an accusation. *Did you not eat those beets with a fork,* you asked, *because it touched my mouth*? *Don't be silly,* I wish I'd replied, *You know me. You don't have to fear my rebuke. Feel no shame.* I wish I hadn't gotten mad and thrown disbelief back into your face, shouting, *How could you think that of me?* If only I'd taken a step back. If only you'd framed your question in a way that would have allowed me to see your own misgivings with where your mind went in its hyper-vigilance as you watched me put down my fork and pick at my beets with my hands. If only you knew that I love beets until I don't. How something in my mouth goes silvery and weird and then I'm done. You added: *I have to ask because I saw something, and it would be less than strong and brave of me not to bring it up.* But all I could do was see your fear and raise it with anger, which we both know only deepens the divide. I'll say now: I am sorry for not taking you in my arms and whispering quiet assurance in your ear. May we someday soon share a meal, eating with our hands, and pass back and forth choice morsels freely and with good will.

Donut

When I met Matt outside the stadium, "Take Me Out to the Ballgame" was blaring over the speakers. I joked, "All I ask for is to not get hit in the head." Matt looked at me funny and laughed. "You set the bar awfully low." The seats were twenty rows up, directly behind home plate. Matt noted that we had a good chance of not getting hit. He did not know—how could he?—that I had bad luck in this regard. The batter swung and missed. He foul tipped the next pitch down the right-field line. He fouled the next pitch, a fastball, straight back, over the net and up into the stands, ricocheting directly behind us, booming onto the empty metal seats. Matt mumbled, *Damn!* The next pitch careened over the net too, slammed into the roof, and rained down hard about six or seven seats to our right. Matt looked over with a curious smile. The woman sitting a few rows down turned around in her seat: "You're gonna have to move if this keeps up." The next inning much the same. The ball sailed over the net at least three more times. I ran into the woman during the seventh inning stretch, and she put two fingers to her eyes then flicked them in my direction. *I'm watching you*. I purchased an Asheville Tourists hat and a twenty-ounce beer in a super-sized plastic cup, then wound my way back to our seats. The stands were full. The hometown crowd chanted "Donut! Donut! Donut!" in hopes of cashing in on the night's promotion, No Hit Inning. The pitcher retired the side in twelve pitches.

Imminence

It has been my practice to place my first trust in the human voice . . .
—Kevin McIlvoy

Over coffee our conversation veers, as it often does, to the creative process: to the footage of the Beatles killing time in that makeshift studio, straining to come up with material for their contractual swan song—last album, last concert, last hurrah. How they keep grasping for straws, playing lick after lick—Chuck Berry, Chet Atkins, any old song—as they crack mean jokes and mug for the camera. How they stalking-horse the sycophants to hide their disgust for one another, for themselves. George ever the jilted lover to John and Paul's soured musical romance. Only Ringo patient enough to wait around for the half-inspired chord, the melody line, the quirky lyric floating in Paul's flytrap mind. *Absorptive intelligence* is how you put it. And then how Yoko steals the show over and over, trickster spirit embodied—John's protector and electric prod, both. How we want to be there when Billy Preston walks in, key to the locked door glimmering inside his easy smile. Then off to our respective days—you to play tennis, me to meet our son about his car. It's not until the next morning that I learn you are dead, felled by a heart attack. I don't know what to say. How could your mellifluous voice be stilled? Sly laugh smothered. Brother Voice, I already miss you.

Zaddik

He was a sunburst of a man, a giant generous spirit tuned to everything giving and communal and good. A man of hugs. A man happy sitting around a table of well-cooked food passed from hand to hand. Head of all seders, young boy in the corner seat with a question. Breaker of bed, dancer of dancers. Quiet reciter of prayer, bold song-belter, singing voice dancing on Hebraic waves. Teacher with an impish smile flashing with playful deviousness. One who happily joins in the necessary work, hands plunged in soil. Proud grandpa. Adoring husband. The father we all wish for. Builder of abodes. Man whose life broadcasts out like a grand Hollywood romance. Man not afraid to have friends in low places. Lover of the raised glass. Whose students remember him and praise him and mourn his passing. Friend in need. Who, when he listens to you, makes you feel like you're the only person in the world. A boy who found freedom in Sephardic streets. Clasper of elbows. Righteous man. Mensch. Zaddik. All this shared today as we come together to honor and bury and pray for this great man—testimony, remembrance, grief, all our love for Hanan and Goldie. At the freshly filled grave, the rabbi speaks the old words. Our duty now to go forward and, as much as is possible, bring this man's noble nature out into the world. Which will be a better place for it.

The Patient Body

The Patient Body & Root Shock

The first shock is the parent's divorce. Only five years old. One day the patient body's father was gone. The patient body waited at the bay window after school. A memory or a figment of the imagination? Fill in the blank. Choose your own adventure. Maybe decisions are like questions given room to become ellipsis. Family history a myth the collective agrees on when offered a false choice. Which makes family photos a kind of barbed wire, strung to keep tumbleweeds from falling off the face of . . . Let's start this again. Root shock predated the patient body's sense of things. It made and unmade. Stripped and filled.

The Patient Body on the Day Everything Changed

The patient body was driving to work on backroads when word came on the morning radio and so imagined a bi-plane's nose bumping into a steel wall and falling to the ground, pesky mosquito. Later, the patient body learned a commercial jet pierced the building, terrorist attack, with another plane arrowing toward the second tower. Almost impossible, but that plane hit its target. Then the first tower collapsed. Removed from screens, sans cellphone, the body still had not taken in a single image. But then, surrounded by colleagues in the lounge, the patient body watched on the television as men and women jumped out of open windows. Saw clouds of rubble, ash-covered people fleeing down streets. Then the second tower went down. Hard to believe now, but the patient body made its way to the classroom and waited for students to show. Many of them did. They sat in a circle for an hour, allowing one another to cry and yell and wonder aloud what their world would be now, and how they might never be able to fit themselves into its new narrative.

The Patient Body Remembers

The patient body remembers the tremor of the head-on collision's impact shimmer-shocking into its breaking frame—from cracked-open feet to split ribcage. Rattling a while then expiring into resonant silence. Breath over breath over breath then release. How many lifetimes ago? How many selves sloughed off? Most days, the event's terrible truth slips by unrecognized, and the patient body lives free of its grasping ghost. On others, triggered by this or that, the patient body replays the accident, lost in the blurry home movie. Over time a voice arises, unbidden, and calls the patient body back to the Now. Reminds the body to step over the ever-widening circles of aftershock. The voice whispers: *Each day out, you must not forget, an excursion*. Whispers: *At each tripping wave, awake.*

The Patient Body & Weightlessness

Not until they wheeled the patient body down the ramp into the warm salt pool, not until it slipped off the highchair, does the body come back to life, upright, circuitry reengaged. The mind drops out of the head and the body dives seal-like into a stream of unencumbered movement. The added saline and heat make the patient body buoyant, weightless. Ecstatic, the body falls again into its steps and teeters forward a few glorious feet: the distance from poolside to poolside, striding and free. The real work comes later, on the mats, between the bars, then up and down the stairs. Nothing new: just two ends of a spectrum. Not until later, walking in the neighborhood, do the two states come together—come together through the body—so that the grind of getting back the body gets subsumed inside the glide of a good groove. Not until the patient body has been thoroughly humbled.

The Patient Body Walks the Dog

About a year after the accident, on one of those blustery early spring mornings—a storm heading north at a crawl, dragging a shawl of rain—the neighborhood woke to a power outage. The house was dark and dank. Most likely some sick tree had been unseated by this last push of rain and toppled, swooning, into the open arms of power lines. Regardless, and though it hadn't been long back on its feet, the patient body headed out for a walk with the dogs. The previous night's rain had left pools in the golf path potholes. The back nine empty of golfers; the first quartet soon to be carting up the hill. The dog bounded out of a patch of dewy rough, a golf ball cupped in her mouth, then rolled in the grass. It felt good to be back in something resembling a normal groove. But then, feet aching, the patient body had to mince down the eighteenth, slippery in its bare patches. Sirens rose up on River Road: first an ambulance, then a fire truck, then two cop cars speeding toward the crash site barely discernible through the break in the trees. By the time the patient body got down to the clubhouse, a line of diverted cars was driving up the lane, forcing him over into the scrub. The heart lifted up into the patient body's throat as it worked to keep the dog tight on its leash. Head ducked in fear when someone cried, "Fore!"

The Patient Body Disguised as a Church Fire

As in, *He is a walking church fire.* As in, someone left rags in the bin without flushing out the spirits. As in, fire trucks from three counties converged in the center town night to aim hoses at a top hat of smoke spouting from the old building's head. As in, fire shimmying up the drywall like a fast-moving cancer, flashing flames inside sweating window frames. As in, lucky no one ended up dead.

The Patient Body Looks at Itself in a Funhouse Mirror

It's a no-brainer: the patient body looks in the mirror and sees what it can see inside the fog. And there it is! Or at least it thinks it could be. Why not? A decade vanishing in quicksilver. *I'm back!* Really, it's easy as 1-2-3. It's the aftermath that's difficult. All the usual paparazzi buzzing outside when the body brings out the trash. Proposals for marriage. In time, the patient body won't remember how it ever forgot itself. Hasn't it been here the whole time? Maybe not. Maybe the body is a stand-in for someone else. Or something else is standing in for the body.

The Patient Body as Jekyll & Hyde

The patient body had two selves. One wanted to know how the other lived; the other in the dark about the one. How could this discrepancy be? It took 100-mile-an-hour force to knock the arm off that broken record. It took another 100,000 hours to return to center. All of it worth it. All of it just fine. At best: the one and the other had chosen this body, this single life, in which to take up residence. Though it sucks to be tethered to a husk sloughed off eons ago; to be known by its visage, its sordid wardrobe. *There he goes*, they say. *The bastard*. The patient body not that guy anymore, really, though the more the explanation the further the fall in estimation. Better go along with the charade, a spy inside enemy lines. Wait long enough and neither will be recognizable—two old men lost inside mirrors. In this endless undercover Op, expect little to nothing of acquaintances. The patient body knows which friends are true and treats them as the royalty they are.

The Patient Body Wanders into Applebee's

The patient body's mistake is to take a seat at the horseshoe's grip, open tables surrounding in a fan. An hour to kill and a beer calling for the back of its throat. A wolf howls nearby and a woman the next seat over fishes out her phone. *Uh-oh*, the patient body whispers. *Don't let this one in. If she starts talking, you're stuck.* The patient body needs time to think. Or not to think. Meant to say *drink*. The check arrives as a man stinking of booze sinks down between them—Wiley E. Coyote coming to stop on "X" marking the spot on an outcrop of rock, broken-off tip suspended in midair like an anvil, waiting for the actor to hit his mark before it drops.

The Patient Body Gets an MRI

Let's talk, now that the patient body is freed from this giant tube, about all the ways torture can be articulated and all the permutations one goes through to keep one's cool. And *goes through* should be *endures*. And by *cool* what is meant is not losing it. Where did the idea come from that this will take fifteen minutes? Turns out more like forty-five. Or so says the young woman who pushes the button. Too late, the body starts sliding in. And what was said to be a series of loud bangs and alarm bells in reality are a clockwork-orangian array of techno-jack-hammer rhythms pulsed into the brain at maximum volume—one series switched out for another between brief, sadistically calming periods of sound wash (as if held up lightly by clouds) and precipitated by curious animal-in-the-wall knocks. Add to this the tight squeeze, the headgear locking in the body as the warm blanket slowly transforms into a hair suit. The patient body wasn't ready for the gestalt of it, the pure sensory overload. Nor the inability to drown out the cacophony, nor the panic rising within the body. All stratagems ditched—reciting poems, tournament seedings, the names of old girlfriends—and in their place breaths get slowly counted. Though that leads to breathing *too* deep which walks the body to the precipice edge of hyper-ventilation. Nothing to do but start counting minutes: 1 to 60 . . . five-minute blocks. Which brings the body up to the thirty-minute mark where it is conveyor-belted back into the light for an IV hookup. *Fifteen minutes to go*, chirps the technician before disappearing from view. Back inside. Back to counting. There is one interval where the cosmic pulse matches the counting and the body rides its wave for a while before it subsumes the body, encompassing breaths, obscuring numbers, sending the mind down a rabbit hole of boundless panic, cartoon script floating . . . 47 . . . 48 . . . 49 . . . Reaching up, grabbing hold, hand over fist to sixty, resting on its wobbly platform then jumping back into the counting, riding on home, where morning light rises over the horizon and the moon rotates out of view. The body once again stuck behind the wheel of the crashed car, once again released from its hold.

The Patient Body & the Night Nurse

The night nurse knows to talk to the patient body. To ask the body to take slow, deep breaths, calm its mind if it can. And the patient body, in its way, knows to respond. And so it goes, late into the night, the nurse calming the body. The patient body looking up, mute, expectant. At some point, the night nurse, sensing its distress, starts talking to the body. The patient body thinks it may have conjured the night nurse. How else does it know to address the nurse in the second person so that when the body does speak it can speak in the first? What the nurse says to the body is simple. *Stay calm. Mind your breaths.* Sometimes the nurse can sense the patient body is lost in a tangle of visions and so answers its wild searchlight eyes with *Let's not go there now.* The nurse places a damp towel to its forehead, sings childhood songs, as the patient body climbs its ladder breath up and up toward sleep.

The Patient Body Walks Along the Lakeshore

> You load yourself up with beauty
> then you bring that out in your art.
> —Piet Oudolf

In amongst a gallery of scrub brush, the patient body is transformed into an undulating clump of stalks. A red-tailed hawk circles back and, as it banks over the lake, releases a prehistoric complaint, proving to the patient body that what it feels rarely lines up with the effect of its physical presence on the surrounding environment. The end of June approaches. The blueline remains, windy day or calm, marking where sandbar ends and lake becomes deep and cold. Within the hour it will be officially warm. A butterfly flits inside a miniature forest of swamp grass—a single lily a day away from uttering its name. Hopping from treetop to treetop, a pair of crows shadow the patient body's path, letting the body know it has entered their zone and should soon leave it. The tinkle of a bell allows bikers to pass. Up ahead a runner and her dog bob up and down. The trail empty on the way out fills with recreational use on the way back. The job of art, the patient body muses, is to make one see things one hasn't noticed. To make anew the things one has seen. Which means a good walk should match the pace of the body's abiding attention. Or so it seems to the body here, this morning, on this walking path lipping the lakeshore.

The Patient Body at the Brewpub for an Afternoon Beer

The patient body sits in the center of an empty table, elbows akimbo, back to open garage door, slumped a little like a Hopper nighthawk. Head down, the patient body ink-drops thoughts onto a slowly-filling page. Not waiting for an old friend, or a long-ago lover whose gait is recognizable in the footsteps rounding the corner. Not flirting with the woman at the counter but taking the pint and finding a seat. The patient body has learned to stay quiet and watch the world spin on its merry-go-round axis. There's a paperback to read or the latest *Mountain Xpress* left folded on a neighboring chair, half a crossword to fill in. No longer trying to interpret old signs for hidden meaning nor add graffiti to the bathroom stall. Instead, draining the beer and walking out into the day—re-set and blank as the sun, brainpan empty—aching feet walking the body, step by step, in the direction of the car.

The Patient Body Sits on the Back Porch and Listens

The construction workers across the way blast ranchera songs. The patient body can hear them chatting between songs, though the midsummer canopy hides them from view. A light mist of rain. A gulley runs between, bound on both sides by potholed roads. The music, the voices, the mist, the morning cars carrying their passengers home from work, from school—all of it seeps together into a single soundtrack. A crow calls in the distance. Judging by the light roar down the hill, a truck passes by on River Road. Now another. One of the workers drops a stack of wood. Two squirrels bicker in the overstory. The body knows that the rain has started to pick up by the brush-snare stirred on the drumhead leaves. Someone turns up the music across the way, then someone (the foreman?) snaps it off.

Neighbor

All the Places Since Lockdown I Don't Go Anymore

There's the airport, to start. I must confess I don't miss it, though its means to an end would be nice about now. Downtown cafés, with their corner tables and aural clatter and espresso machine hiss. Bookstore aisles, nightclubs; anywhere where people gather. I stopped going to laundromats years ago, and don't take the bus, but I'd think twice entering either. Same for bathhouses, brothels, drug dens. Not my scene, but I miss them too. And loud newsrooms, slaughterhouses, assembly lines: it's lucky I can forego them. Bars, of course. A few will sell you a pint in a plastic cup and let you sit out back. I've done that, bundled up from the cold, it's lonely fun. It's the going out, really, I crave. Having a thing to do. It'll come back; I'll be patient. But what if these places, the swirling worlds they contain, aren't the same upon return? What then?

Double Masked

What are we so afraid of? Why is it so hard to move out of our comfort zone? And how can it be that taking a small risk often yields such great reward? These are the questions I keep asking, here deep inside the pandemic realm, in this world where an elderly neighbor works outside in her yard, double-masked, keeping a large distance between us when we chat. She has already lost a husband. There is much for her to watch out for, fret over. One of the few Black women in a predominantly white neighborhood, she lives adjacent to a public golf course fairway, at the crest of a hill, where cars speed past and errant drives land at her feet. Still, there she is most days, out in the yard tending to a patch of grass with stubborn resolve. She looks up when I call out and sometimes stops to wave or chat. Occasionally, I see her driving her husband's old truck back from the store, her face hidden from view by the mask, only her bespectacled eyes peeking out. I can't tell if she looks afraid, or steely, or just plain tired. Once, she came out to the side of the road and bent down to pat my dog, mumbling something into her ear. Then she stood up, stretched, and gave me a smile that wrinkled her eyes. I write these lines to her, for her, with her in mind. Or, at least, this is my goal, the news all around me sounding the alarm.

Seeing Bears

Bears have taken up residence in our neighborhood. Sightings are a common occurrence. Look up and there's a bear at the feeder or eating the Halloween candy off a neighbor's porch. Mama Bear and three teenage cubs materializing, one by one, out of the hedge—a conga line of surprise. Mama swiveling her head and sniffing. One young cub stood and swayed, a dancing man, then slipped back down into its hulking self. Mama waded into the trees at driveway's end, sniffing back. *We don't need you.* Then they were gone. It seems a new family unit roams these corridors every spring: they come down from the mountains, cross the main road, then take up residence on the public golf course. They winter in the ravine down from our house. I ran into an adolescent one morning coming around a bend, the bear atop a steep embankment above. A brief pause then it bum-rushed me, charging forward, snorting and growling as I back-pedaled with the dogs tight on leash and went all out cartoon-mode, *whoa-whoa.* Then there is Mama hunched in the lower branches of a giant oak. Before I can react, the dog bolts forward: I take the leash's jolt in my shoulder, doing my best to drag the domestic beast back. The bear crouches on all fours, back humped up, calmly observing as I shock to its presence. We remain like this for a while, taking each other in. It takes a moment before I spy first one, then two, then three, four bear cubs spread out in the branches above, as if in a children's book, little thought-bubbles of worry rising from Mama's massive head.

Dementia

No one gets up after death.
—*Rosencrantz and Guildenstern Are Dead*

Each day I meet a different Betty. Each time not a new facet but a whole new diamond nicked up, cataract clouded. One day Betty is lucid, fully engaged, curious to know of all the family hiccups. (She used to be a psychotherapist and so listens well and gives wise consul.) Then another too much information, or news that is itself too much, elicits a light flailing of her hands and an urgent *Oh no* or a *That's not good*, and the wild look in Betty's eye tells me I am disturbing her new world view. The one in which her dog Dancer is now "The Dog," and her old house in our neighborhood, now sold, "That Place." I've overloaded her. One day she seems to want to leave her new living arrangement, seems to believe she has some say in the matter. Though the next she says "we" when she talks about the overworked and understaffed staff. She has lost all interest in getting back into town. It seems to her a far-off country with borders nearly impossible to cross without the correct papers. I bring her copies of *The New Yorker* and, on one occasion, a potted plant. The staff thinks I am her son. Betty will forget my name, how long it has been since I've last come. *I have been worrying about you*, she says. *I was concerned you'd lost track of me.* Am I her son, her neighbor, or an old friend from her time in Vienna? It changes depending on the occasion. Which begs the question: How many versions of *me* am I dragging to our meetings? How much of *me* is missing?

Balance

Her back is to me. His face is surprisingly boyish for an old man. His son holds him lightly by the elbow with two stabilizing fingers. The man's smile has transfixed the woman; I can tell even with her back turned. She wears the store's blue vest and is supposed to be helping customers. I don't want to interrupt, it isn't busy, I have no place to go. I stand there watching her gesture and laugh at the old man's stories. I can tell by the son's expression the man has done this a hundred times. He isn't going to stop anytime soon, so I remain there for another minute, playing my part. The old man asks her age. She answers, "Seventy-eight." The son *tssks* the father for his audacious question. The old man takes it one step further. "You know what they say, 'If you ask a woman her age and she gives it to you . . .'" "She'll give you anything," the clerk finishes, laughing. She grasps the old man with both arms. I tap her on the shoulder when the man starts talking again—about the book he's written about his life, brother of a famous actor. I am worried we are headed down a path we'll not soon return from. The woman turns immediately—spell broken—and apologizes. The son gives his father a light pinch on the elbow. And they head out, both smiling, the old man's face still surprisingly boyish, eyes gleaming. I go outside with my receipt and wait for someone to unlock the cabinet. Eventually the woman steps outside and thanks me for my patience. She seems much younger than 78, though her face shows her age. I should thank her back, but just then a young woman appears with a key; I haul the propane tank to the car. What shall I be thankful for? Maybe for the sheer entertainment value of it all. Or maybe by the way the old man, as well-timed as a seasoned comic, said: *You have to turn me to the wall to stop me from talking.* How he turned to an imaginary wall for a beat before turning back, all smiles, letting his son help him regain his balance.

Wave

The boy who lives up the hill won't look at me, can't seem to look at me, at least not for more than a second before turning away, back to his private world I glimpse only in the fluttering of hands and the quiet words he speaks to himself and only himself. I call out *Hello!* and wave just the same, giving him a quick smile then looking away myself, out of respect. I know what he lives with it, know that I don't have access to his world and don't need to. His mom has thanked me for this ritual. *He likes being outside*, she says. I ask after him when I see her on her own. *This new school he's going to helps*, she says. *He's a good boy*, I say, hoping that my interest is seen less as nuisance and more as neighborly good will. I don't see him this evening as I stroll with the dogs down the hill. There's a little chill in the air and the wind rustles the trees, especially the small Japanese Maple that stands in their yard, as if a small squall has dropped down and brought the tree to life. As I pass by closer, I spy the boy inside the tree, sitting in amongst its nest of leaves. He is shaking the branches lightly, causing the young tree to undulate all around him. I don't call out—don't have to—just a small smile. For tonight it is he who waves to me.

Satin Doll

If you have lived in town long, you have surely heard him playing his saxophone on the street corner. He's not all that good anymore, but you can tell that Bobby was once not half bad. He played with Marvin, he'd tell you, and I half believe him. For the last few years, he's been playing in front of Whole Foods, and lately I've been buying him a pizza slice and bottle of lemonade and sitting down to talk. He's a sweet guy, very personable and polite, but it's not until he knows that I like jazz that he really opens up. He asks if I know Stanley Turrentine. I nod. He picks up his horn and plays the opening melody of a song. Smiling mischievously, he asks: "What's that?" "Sugar?" I've just heard the song on the radio. He laughs, his boyishly handsome face radiating good nature. It doesn't hurt I know the name of the Ramsey Lewis album he's trying to remember—*Sun Goddess*—that has Earth, Wind & Fire as the backing band. This afternoon he's lamenting the deaths of some old friends back in Detroit and DC. He wanted to visit them but is too late. "I lost them both," he says. I have recently lost two old friends—both mentors—and can sympathize. "I'm eighty," he says. "So, I know I'm lucky. Maybe it's in the genes." He asks me to write down my number (now for the third time) and reiterates his desire to come onto my radio show. "I've got stories," he says. "Anytime," I tell him and mean it. As I walk back to my car, he starts in on "Satin Doll" and, for the first few bars at least, plays it with brio and a bright, clear tone.

Citizen

In the Parliament of the Common Man

In the parliament of the common man, men hunker around the lean fire of a newspaper and talk of tyrants and the politics of power. An electric current pulses around a ragged circle of pointing fingers, eager faces. In the parliament of the common man, a pick-up game rumbles to life, and someone offers, *It's a shame about O.* A young man asks, *What's a shame?* The ball ripped from his hands. *Just how hard I'm gonna dunk on your sorry ass.* In the parliament of the common man, Robert's Rules do not apply. No ritual goat dance, no show of hands. Only the heated exchange of small groups. *How did we let this happen? You had it coming! What will happen to us now?* In the parliament of the common man, men and women stand in protest, shouting out spondee slogans; in a darkening room a cabal of old white men, quiet and savage, hungrily unravel the fabric of decency and good will.

News

January 8, 2021

I'm done with this crowd. They who pretend down is up, that looting and lynching are god given. Delusion raised to shrill song. I'm done with being done. Done caring, done fearing, pretending I accept any of it, anymore, ever. Sleep doses desire. Hurt cries for withdrawal. Let us engage one another who don't lie, that don't require old nightmares remain in place. I am talking to myself, my selves. I mean today. Now.

February 2, 2021

You're acting like a child, the officer says. To which she responds, *I am a child.* The only "adult in the room," a nine-year-old girl surrounded by cops about to pepper spray her. A nine-year-old Black girl who studies show is three times more likely to be treated with violence than white girls. And the classroom is a squad car. And the assignment: get help for a girl in trouble. And her mother is the teacher, but pepper spray is the switch, the stick, the fist; and the cops are schoolyard bullies getting off on her fear. And we have become bystanders, and our anger and our indignation turn to bile in our throats. And the girl in most need tells us all what we need to hear. *I am only a child.*

Stalemate

The pump's not working so I go inside and pay. There's a logjam up at the front counter. A middle-aged man dressed in a pair of worn slacks and a baseball jacket loudly admonishes an older woman behind the counter, who seems to be on the phone. "I just wanna pay for my gas and go. Let me pay." The woman puts her hand over the receiver. "My manager's gonna call the cops." *Uh-oh, not that nightmare.* A second employee, staring blankly as if she's seen it all before, waves me over. I swipe my card and watch as the first woman puts down the phone. "Don't be so rude," she says to the man who visibly stiffens at her words. "The next time I come here," he speaks at her, enunciating each word, "I am going to make you cry." The woman laughs. "The only two men in this world who can make me cry are my husband and my son." She retreats to the back as she says this. Maybe they've had this argument before. The cashier hands me back my card then reaches her hand out to the man, palm up, not looking at him. He waits a moment then walks over and hands her the money. "Sorry about that," I say, following the man out, though I am not sure what I am apologizing for. "It's all right. Happens all the time." We reach the gas pump at the same time. "I bet it does." As I wait, I catch a glimpse of a woman scrolling on her phone in the front seat. What are the odds, if the situation had gotten more heated, or if the manager showed up, that the police would have arrived soon after? *Black man at the scene. May have a gun.*

Script Flipped

We've all seen the photograph of the billboard—*Martin Luther King at Communist Training School*—standing in a field somewhere down south. In an act of implied assassination, a dark arrow labeled "King" points at MLK's chest. Today, we have our own virtual fields of incitements—the same old hate speech bubbling inside vigilante gangs and lynch mobs. The same vitriol and spite. And so that photo from our deep-south past returns us to the scene of the crime. Puts us there as mute witness. We're standing on the side of the road, down south to register voters. A truck rolls by and two men in short sleeves stare us down. But I want a different movie. OPEN ON: an empty field baking in the summer heat. No fenced-in outbuildings, no billboards, no passing trucks. CUT TO: Memphis. King is pushed down just as the bullet whizzes by and so survives the attempt on his life. Strike that. Try it without the shooter. INT: King and his entourage have gone inside for a drink. Or EXT: Martin's alone on the balcony, looking up at the stars. He's thinking about his next speech. About what it will take to change the hearts and minds of a country warped by its history. He's composing a love letter to the people. The camera RISES UP into the clouds.

for Van

Electric Fence

On my way to drop off the dogs I pass through the land of Trump signs and Confederate flags. It hasn't always been like this: never simply this or that. Now an old Obama sticker puts a target on my back. Sandra's not out at the fence when I arrive. I have forgotten that horses graze the field so don't notice the wire running atop the long drive's parallel fences. In such close quarters, dogs on leash, awkward with the latch, I sway to the left. *Zap.* A shock runs across my chest and shoots out my arm. I shout *What the fuck!* and throw up my hands. I look around in fury. And Sandra appears, standing there chuckling. *It's a kinder, gentler shock,* she says, opening the gate to let the dogs through. *It could have been worse.*

Unhoused

Out walking the dogs. The man wearing a giant beat-up backpack asked me how to get to Walmart. He'd been, he'd said, on a bus for thirteen days. Had started out in Oregon, was robbed in Colorado Springs. The man showed me his scarred arm. He said, *People think I am a tweaker.* That people were afraid of him because he was homeless. One of his eyes drifted up and left. Ragged mustache, hair close-cropped. When I gave the man directions—it was about a mile and a half walk—he started to cry. Unsure of what to do, I wished him luck and walked on. Once home, not satisfied with my behavior, I grabbed my car keys and wallet, making sure I had a twenty. I found the man not far up the road and waited for him at a bend. When he arrived at my window, I offered him a ride. Again, the man started to cry. *My blood sugar's low,* he apologized. *I have the number of a man who has promised me work,* he said, though his phone had been taken from him, as well as $3,000 worth of cash and belongings. That's how the man put it, "belongings." I pulled out two masks from the glove compartment and asked the man to wear a mask. We put the masks on at the same time. When we got to Walmart, the man asked if there was a McDonald's nearby. I said I thought there was one inside and gave him the name of an organization that helped men and women in this situation. I hadn't thought to bring their number and, in my rush, had forgotten to bring my phone. The man copied the information down on a small piece of paper that he plucked out of an old leather wallet. He said he had a lot of different skills but that he'd pick up dog shit in his bare hands to make money. Before he went inside, the man told me that he used to live in the area, out in Hendersonville, that his brother and his wife lived there, but he didn't have their number. I wished the man luck a second time and handed him the twenty. Then I got into my car and drove off. The man had told me his name, but I forgot it by the time I arrived home.

Man Snoring on Plane, Dallas to Charlotte

> . . . but it's business in America, a country where
> I can't afford the price of my own vigilance.
> —Allison Joseph, "Some of My Best Friends are White People"

A young woman in a window seat across the aisle is snoring. A few passengers smile and laugh. When I look up a little later, the woman's still snoring, joined by a man one row up, also snoring. More people turn their heads and look to see where the noise comes from. It's as if someone's slurping a smoothie through a straw. The mood remains light. I return to my book, looking up again after a while: the young woman's awake but the man is still snoring. The women beside me start talk disparagingly about the man. So too the men in front. I rise out of my seat: the man snoring is Black and everyone around the man is white, just like me. As if on cue, the man stops. I turn back to my book. When it's time to prepare for landing, I put my book away. The man's snoring again. No one tries to wake him. The people around me seem disgusted by the man. It's in their body language (the teen sitting next to the man shrinks back when he stretches out in sleep) and in their speech. One teen to another: *It's like you're being violated.* Their disdain comes across clear as day. And when the plane comes to a stop and everyone stands and he still doesn't wake, suddenly the white people surrounding him, now standing over him, start to make belittling comments. *Maybe he's actually awake, and he's listening to us . . . At least it's not me.* There's a Black woman a few rows behind, standing ramrod still, face plastered with grief. I say, *I hate this* and push past the passengers in the aisle and attempt to wake the man. He doesn't stir. The line prepares to move forward, so I turn to the teen hanging over his chair and hiss: *Try to wake him. See if he's okay.* The kid's eyes open wide as if he has woken out of a stupor. He leans in, gives the man a hard shake. The line ahead starts moving. I return to my seat and grab my bag. The woman leans in and says, *Thank you for trying.* Just then the man wakes, stretching out his arms. As he rises to exit the plane, everyone around him is in the act of turning away.

Traveler

At the Frida Kahlo Museo, Playa del Carmen

She was dying her whole life.
—Andrés Henestrosa

A day spent chasing our equilibrium. Driving into a new city unsure of where to go, who gives way to whom. A half hour search and the rental squeezed into a space a foot larger than the car; everything loaded into the trunk then making our way to the strip, slipping into the tidal pull of bodies, the cacophony of the city flowing over us. Avery disappeared through a curtain of blaring hip-hop; Ali in search of a jewelry shop. I ordered a lunchtime beer, watched the sewage truck suck up its week full of slag and muck; it blasted an airplane roar, a dirge note in my brain. When it finally quit, I could hear chimes from a second story, a pair of birds up in a tree, and the whistle of a young man on his bike calling a friend forward. Ali returning with news of a museum just few blocks up; Avery wanting to find the vape store passed on the way in, hoping to buy a glass bong that will surely break on the trip home. Like a dog watcher stretched opposite directions by stubborn noses, I floated in the middle—needing out of the searing sun—before making my way to the little side-street *museo*. It took a moment to focus on the wall up front, a life-size image of Frida staring out, one of her early self-portraits with monkey. And a few more to realize the show was homage dressed up in the garb of natural history. Perfect for Frida. The story of a heroic life—a little Joan of Arc, a dash of Warhol chic, and a whole lot of *duende*. Still, it was hard to settle into the flow with Avery out floating in among the bad-things-happen possibilities, looking to score weed on 4/20, desperate for adventure not sanctioned by the tourist board. Even when he showed up in the lobby armchair, hunched over phone, all teenage smolder, I struggled to slow down and just look. I drifted through the exhibit, checking in with Avery, checking with Ali. The best I could do was take snapshots of the captions and look at the posters of the later paintings.

It was when I came upon the tragic accident that almost killed Frida that I woke up out of my stupor. The text on the wall read: *Many have said that her accident was fatal, but she didn't die because her destiny was to survive, and thus endure an ordeal of pain*. It told of a young Frida being javelined by a metal pole while sitting in a trolley car, pinned to the ground. Her words: *The crash thrust us forward and the handrail went through me like a stake through a bull.*

On the Lee Highway, Staunton, VA, to Johnson City, TN

Interstate 81 traffic has backed up onto its exit ramps. On the drive north I'd spied the shadow road ghosting the interstate strip—crisscrossing over and under bridges all the way to Staunton. Why not jump onto it now and sidestep all this gridlock? Which becomes: why not stay on it a little longer and enjoy the near empty road, the lovely countryside flowing all around us? Cows posing in fields. Passing into and through little towns, as the joke goes, in a blink. Which brings us to the North Star, right here on the side of the road, and one of those all-American diner lunches you can still get almost anywhere if you look hard enough or live there. Sitting around basic tables, surrounded by locals talking quietly over their meals. No bill, just the amount called out from the waitress stand. *Have a goodun* then back on the road. But now, with a taste of the sharp piquancy of the unplanned, we're unwilling to turn back to the standard way. Why not drive until dark and find a hotel with restaurant and a bar? What's waiting at home, anyway? Another hour driving down the nostalgia of backroads. The road's history is rich, and long, and we begin to dream of taking it all the way to San Francisco. There's one passage up and up into the foothills—the center of this adventure, its pivot—that has the car slipping through shaded hollers, banking into undulating curves. A few more hours of this backroad wandering then finally pulling in beside the Birthplace of Country Music Museum. Dinner then a nightcap on the hotel's rooftop bar. Waking to the train whistle at two, so loud it feels like I'm in a sleeping car, lolling in the dark. Down for breakfast now, ready to get back on the road—two more hours to get up and over the mountains into Asheville—the streets wet with the night's rain, blue sky rolling in from the north dragging clouds up over the mountains—a half full tank, the open road. There's one last stretch of Highway 11, over to Johnson City, before getting on the future 26, that has us climbing foothills, then we're up into the old mountains, car buffeted by wind, road twisting up through the peaks; all of a sudden, up and over Sam's Gap, 3,700 feet above sea level, now driving down the stunningly engineered road past first one then another emergency pull off, thick sand folded tightly in order to bring the mammoth runaway eighteen-wheelers to a ragged, abrupt stop.

Walking Walden Pond, Its Paths Now Fenced In By Wire

If Thoreau dropped down into my body like some alien bodhisattva and inhabited it this afternoon, he'd not allow himself such a restricted ramble inside this corridor of wire fencing. Nor would he start at the main beach, nor follow the path up to the cabin site, falling in line behind tourist families. (To see what, a copy of a copy?) He'd argue, no doubt, that this faux cabin was the spot *furthest* from the spirit of the place. He'd swerve away from the tourist trap, lifting up his arms and letting go a Whitmanesque yawp. How un-Thoreauvian to make a prison of a stroll. Henry would prefer the walk that heads away from the pond, cross lots to Freeman's Hill, where the black families live, formerly squatters like him, now landowners on the outskirts farming on rock and tired soil. No sanctuary pond but instead a little privacy and a good view down into Concord when the trees are bare. It's what we do here in this teetering democracy: we turn our paradises into museums and mausoleums. The only true wildness I glean the whole ramble round is when I take off my shoes and wade into the water; is when I stall alongside the train tracks after the train has come through. How we love being on the water, how we thrill at the train whistle. Not wilderness we seek, but a keen sense of wildness inside the commerce of the moment.

for DG, JL & TRC

Ghost Tourist

I've walked through this old town countless times before and felt like a ghost slipping in and out of time, with no real connection to the present but a light, tenuous grounding inside uneven footfalls on cobblestones. I was there only because my reflection echoed in the storefront windows. I feel a little like that this drizzly morning, though something has shifted subtly—more tourist now than ghost—that becomes evident as I walk. The only way to characterize this sensation is to say that something—inner make-up more than just mood; temperament in its rawest state, a little agitated, senses on high alert—has allowed me to reside in both the past and the present simultaneously. I am the white-haired fifty-something guy *and* the preteen rushing out of David Cohen's house down into his backyard driveway to shoot hoops. As I wait at the corner for the light to change, allowing a pedestrian to pass, my eyes nearly get gouged out by her low-hanging umbrella. I turn away, now facing an imprint of a burned down building left on the adjacent brick three-story, its upper windows knocked out. In my mind's eye, both buildings remain, windows intact, and I'm standing on top of the flat roof with my bohemian brothers and sisters ill-advisedly tossing a frisbee back and forth and drinking beers. Thirty years dissolve in an instant. Earlier, I passed The Press Room, an English-style pub we used to live beside back in late '70s. I can remember poignantly the nights spent in that smoky, dark cavern while our mother, a recently divorced young woman, hung out with her actor friends. My brother and I staying with her in the two-room walk-up next door. I can almost make out my seven-year-old self peering out from the smudgy window, though now the pristine panes are filled with beauty salon ads. And there's the old church graveyard that me and my buddy used to slip into, passing a joint back and forth; and the Athenaeum in the square, where the old poet shelved books and wrote his penny poems. And, just now, stopping in recognition at a street corner residence, it takes a while to recall the face of the quiet young man who I washed dishes with weekends at Café Petronella. I peer into the dusty windows and smell woodsy incense burning on the mantel, Brian Eno's *My Life in the Bush of Ghosts* spinning on the stereo. Where did that young man go? How can it be that he's been here all along, trapped inside me?

—Portsmouth, NH

On the Fire Road, Between Ponds, Wellfleet

> These houses were on the shores of a chain of ponds, seven in number . . .
>
> —Thoreau, *Cape Cod*

I canoed out to the other end of Long Pond the previous evening—turning the large metal canoe around so to be sitting in what used to be the bow, placing bricks on the floor of what used to be the stern—but this morning I want to get there on foot. I've been told there's another, smaller pond—Dyer Pond—a short ways away: just follow the old dirt fire road along its meandering path. I step over the slouching chain—you might get your car down this wild lane but just barely, and slowly—and wind my way along the path through the quiet, dew-tinged conifers. I run into a few walkers, most with their dogs, but in the main I'm on my own, free when I arrive to stand at pond's edge, birds noisy in the bushes, to watch a thin line of fog haunt the pond's far corner. I've not heard the term "kettle ponds" before and don't know this network of ponds here on the Cape was created by retreating glaciers. (Shame on me!) An old friend who lives in town tells me there is a pond—on how to get there he is silent—where at a friend's cabin Thoreau gathered material for his Cape Cod sketches. The other night, on Long Pond, an osprey soared overhead, circling round for good measure, diving dramatically down toward the placid water. A patch of yellow-green marsh grass swayed quietly back and forth in the shallows, exposed tips a coat bristling inside slowly extinguishing sunlight. This morning—here, now—the trails underfoot are underlaid with dune sand and crosscut by gnarled tree roots slick to tread. I can easily keep going, ambling my way to the next pond, and the next, but a cup of coffee has my name on it and a group back at the rental house will soon be heading for the seashore. How content—and privileged—can one man be?

Hemingway Home, Key West, FL

> An intelligent man is sometimes forced
> to be drunk to spend time with his fools.
> —Ernest Hemingway

You'll want to slip past the long line of tourists. Flash your invisible "writer" badge and the old man at the gate, susceptible to this easy Jedi mind-trick, will wave you through. Nod at the hostess on the front porch steps as if you know one another well and follow the group into the foyer. Take a quick walk through the upstairs rooms, if you'd like, then come down and peek into the dining room. Or skip the house tour altogether: there's nothing in there beyond standard house & garden wares. How could there be? Ignore the plethora of six-toed cats lounging in tropical shade as you head to the back corner of the compound; there you will find Hemingway's writing studio floating like a moon above an aquamarine pool. Don't expect to find anything of value up in the great man's writing room, not even the typewriter, though there *is* something to peering into that cage that serves as gentle reminder of what's really at stake. Make sure to end up poolside. Go ahead, take off your shoes and stick your tired legs into the cold water. Allow the scene to blossom in front of your eyes. The drunk writer lurching into a lounge chair. The bored beauty painting her toes in the shade. The sweating agent with papers to sign. The murderous butler under the banyan leaves muttering terse notes to self while one of Papa's children lies face down in the sun, encased by a slowly expanding cocoon of wet concrete, shivering.

Up at Artillery Hill, Fort Wordon

When my brother comes here, he climbs the hill and takes photographs with his camera phone, mountaingoating around the abandoned barracks on the hunt for abstract shots of graffiti, discolored walls, peeling paint, ancient-looking stone-circle imprints. He takes the ferry back to the city and goes to his studio and paints the images onto canvas. Crops the shots first, making sure he gets the right balance and feel. If my son were here, he'd be climbing all over these great bone fortresses, jumping off walls, disappearing into the eerie cells. Or he'd have done that a few years ago; he's nineteen now, and, who knows, he'd probably slip off and smoke a joint then bushwhack down to the beach and meet back at the room later in the evening smelling of misguided adventure. If Ali were here with me, we'd have found a spot inside one of the lovely shade groves and lain down on a blanket and, after a while, for sure, fallen asleep. But it's just me today; and, come to think of it, I too take snapshots of the ruins, and climb over them—not jumping but walking carefully down the cement stairs—and find a spot under some great uncle tree—the little swallowtail birds swooping by, passing over and through the meadow grass. I startle a pair of deer as I pass down into the woods, and when I turn back from the second doe, only a few feet away, the first deer vanishes. *Poof.*

—Port Townsend, Washington

Artist

The Night Ella Escorted Marilyn through the Front Door of the Mocambo

You heard it wrong: it was Ella ensconced in the front row all week, not Marilyn; and Ella who was joined not by Sinatra and Garland but by Robeson and Horne; and Ella who had her white friend's back, allying for a woman not deemed attractive enough to perform. And it wasn't LA but Kansas City, or Detroit, and there goes the inimitable Ma Rainey, Bessie Smith, and a young Alberta Hunter, drinks all around the four-top. And Marilyn never stopped being Billy Jean and wasn't strumming that damn ukulele or fake whispering but belting out a country blues—hair in a brown bob, shirt and collar, stomping boots—of her ghosted past. While we're at it, "Whites Only" signs never existed, and King's Beloved Community was baked into the Constitution, and John Lewis never had to walk onto that bridge—billy clubs flying in sped-up reverse back into their holsters—cops morphing into regular people like us (all sizes and hues and proclivities), heading out to a field full of banquet tables piled high with steaming food, kegs cooling under trees whose limbs have never been asked to bear black bodies, and a band playing some down-home dirty blues, and everyone up dancing and shouting. Now wouldn't that be something?

Best of the Classic Years

I remember those few hours spent deep in the festival's parking lot: recharging phone battery and self, reclining in the shade of my car, King Sunny Adé blasting on my speaker. Listening to those cuts was like standing inside a spray of liquid sunlight throwing off stipples of drum rhythms and guitar licks. Like walking along a dirt road in the rain, drops bubbling at my feet like johnnycake batter on a griddle. The word *reprieve* floats up in my mind, as does *sanctuary*. Music as temporary bivouac. Music as a tapestry of sounds one wraps around the body or sits under; its netting diffuses the sun, throwing a pattern of shadow across the backs of walls in silent prophesy. My brother turned me onto King Sunny back in '82, I still have the album—*Maa Jo*—which he either gifted me or I stole (the way converts justify devotion) and play it now and again while cooking or shooting hoops in the driveway. I played it on a mixtape once on a Laurel Canyon hardcourt running pick up with hip-hop boys from the suburbs. Turning the boombox up loud and proud as backdrop for our game. Back in that long dusty snake of a festival lot, I wore the music like a flag; and they can tell me I was appropriating the sound, taking someone else's culture as my own, and they'd be right, and they'd be wrong. Both truths in syncopation, both beats laid down for the solo guitar's step dance. I didn't care who came by or what they thought. All I wanted was to get lost in King Sunny's *synchro system* and turn back into my body, that ancient cistern, that broken vessel.

for Major

Seattle Art Fair

Inside this cavernous hall annexed so awkwardly to the sports arena, a phalanx of art lovers shuffle and gawk. Each year the ghost of some new zeitgeist influencer hangs everywhere on the makeshift walls. One year it's Diebenkorn, another Hockney or Frida or Lorna Simpson, now it's Basquiat. In reflexive response, I move to an old-school oil painting unique in its pictorial style and formal technique. I am drawn to the figure in the painting's center: a young man in untucked white shirt, rolled-up baggie pants, bare feet. His being on a high-wire, balancing in air—one leg up, one hand waving while the other grips the balancing pole—feels psychologically right. *Men*, a woman beside you tells a friend, *are showoffs*. In a corner: a cluster of small, ornately framed Klimt and Schiele pieces. The prices are astronomical. Up one long row, down another. Video art seems is the other next big thing. Everywhere I turn, screens. Contrapuntally, one small booth—a gallery from Korea—features abstract prints. When I stop to ask questions, the elegant woman rises from her chair and commends me for my good taste. Flattered, but out of my price range, I turn back into the fray, all of a sudden overloaded—I've had my fill of *viewing*—and make for the exit. The streets are crammed with baseball game foot traffic. How many people going to the game might stop in for a quick look at the art? How many art lovers will grab spare tickets and catch the game? I snap a few random shots on my camera phone: shadows, building reflections. It's what I do after an art show, my sense of looking awakened. I trek up the cement steps perfumed with piss, some song from the art fair speakers echoing in my head. A pigeon drops a tiny shit bomb on my shoulder. Life is good.

Kamasi Washington at the Orange Peel

First the band warms up, thumbing through the first few numbers like a runner letting the body find its groove on the path; then the audience must warm to the band, letting *their* bodies take in the slowly evolving sound as it dresses itself up for the evening; and then, if both the band and the crowd make an extra effort to extend out inwardly into the place where the music fits itself, and the band members locate one another on the stage and retreat from their own roles in order to hear all the other melodies potentialized inside the larger sound, and the audience puts down their needs long enough to find the back entrance of the song—the bar within the bar we always look for—and really tries to *hear* what it is the band is working out—out there, in here. Then, and only then, is there a chance for the whole giant gizmo to resonate, to spiral on its nub and gyrate into the rhythm, to fly off into one long cry of song. That together, all these disparate bodies might just come together and live music's great big Funkadelican spacecraft will rise up, or beam down, or implode in our chests, and take us.

Houdini on the Prowl

. . . at the Vermont Studio Center after a few years away

Some cats seem forever to stalk down alleyways. There's a subtle swagger to their gait, the casual ease of a gunfighter passing down an empty Main Street. Houdini is such a cat—bruiser, mouser, Tom. He follows us as we tour the grounds; stops with us as we note the conspicuous absence of this old barn, that tumbledown garage. Trimming back before regrowth is how one Trustee phrased it; taking deadweight offline is Jim's. Whatever it's called, it's eerie and exhilarating to come upon half-remembered forms floating over freshly seeded plots, like seeing ghosts. When we emerge from a moldy basement of a soon-to-be refurbished building, Houdini slinks down the steps and disappears into the murk. Jim leaves the door open, and we head over to the river: past one old structure and through a newly opened field. I have made my way down here a dozen times, which makes me feel like a tracker coming upon an old scent. This way to the riverbend, that way to the old baseball field now an arboretum. Trevor says he's not been down here since the Covid shutdown. Before turning back, we talk about past complications—board squabbles, founder syndrome, and the like—and share hope for some small portion of healing. We pause at an old carriage barn, now a smoking hut, where I am told an occasional thru hiker sets up camp before being kindly shooed away. The afternoon chill creeps under our shirts. Houdini reappears, cobwebs crowning his head. He watches us for a moment, yawns, then licks his paw.

You Are Who You Are

When you look at Arbus' shots from the '50s and '60s, real people, not freaks, look back at the camera with little affectation. An openness in their posture and in their expression mirrors hers. There is little staring going on, in either direction. More like a direct, almost loving, gaze. *You are who you are, and I love you for it. I am who I am, so love me for it.* The harsh disapproving stare comes from norm culture, straight culture. "I always thought photography was a naughty thing to do," Arbus once said. "That was one of my favorite things about it." Judgment comes from outside from what isn't present inside the intimate moment. Jealousy lurking behind the naming, the degrading, the willful ignorance. What's this staring, this peering in? I say it's desire to be truly oneself, to be captured in such love.

Echoes

A quiet reverberation rings a tiny bell inside your body: an instantaneous bounce on white-washed wall from eye to artwork and back; a synapse firing in the brain jumpstarting the heart rate. You're at the Basquiat show inside a clump of hipsters here to make the scene. You're standing in front of a large yellow canvas roped to a frame. Looking at the cartoon figure is like looking in a mirror. Like spying on a dead man. Not even a canvas but someone's bedspread stretched like goatskin over a large drum or a stiff net ready to receive your soul and send it back into its own body where it does (or does not) belong. Just you again peering into a vessel a thousand associations full. Same goes with the one of Charlie "Bird" Parker wailing away on his alto, also yellow, Bird's eye glaring, and his fingers working invisible keys. Most of Jean-Michael's heroes wear crowns but here Parker is a bird, majestic and wild. You can hear his solos knocking in your head. Later in the evening, at the Blue Note: a quartet of old friends after years reuniting. The drummer's smile is a regular at the bar, drinks all around. Even from cramped seats you can see the love passing back and forth like a pipe, like a poem recited by heart. McBride gives a lecture on insouciance and heckles himself from the back. Mehldau leans into his solos making sure to answer as much as he can of Redmon's runs which are more like leaps and skip-hops; and Blade shoots up out of his seat and turns the cymbals into fireworks, into applause. Heading back to the hotel in an encore of rain, body electric, mind whizzing around like one of Basquiat's imaginary toys, one of those little whims of childhood brought forth into the land of money. *That's all and good night.* It's the body that connects the dots, the body that stores feelings; the body that knows when to snap the picture through its camera-eye. Your eyes scan and scan, the brain grabs onto all the shiny things it can while the patient body takes the echo, like the wall, and throws it back.

Biographical Note

Sebastian Matthews is the author of the memoir-in-essays *Beyond Repair: Living in a Fractured State* and the hybrid collection *Beginner's Guide to a Head-On Collision*. His other publications include two books of poems, the memoir *In My Father's Footsteps*, the collage novel *The Life & Times of American Crow*, and a collaboration with photographer Charter Weeks entitled *Travelogue*. He works as a writing coach and leads workshops for the Great Smokies Writing Program in Asheville, NC.

www.ingramcontent.com/pod-product-compliance
Lightning Source LLC
Jackson TN
JSHW082114040225
78413JS00003B/3

* 9 7 8 1 6 3 6 2 8 2 4 4 2 *